SPOTLIGHT ON NATURE

TIGER

MELISSA GISH

CREATIVE EDUCATION · CREATIVE PAPERBACKS

Published by Creative Education and Creative Paperbacks
P.O. Box 227, Mankato, Minnesota 56002
Creative Education and Creative Paperbacks are imprints of The Creative Company
www.thecreativecompany.us

Design by Chelsey Luther; production by Joe Kahnke
Art direction by Rita Marshall
Printed in the United States of America

Photographs by Alamy (dpa picture alliance archive, Juniors Bildarchiv GmbH), Dreamstime (Vaclav Volrab), Getty Images (Aprison Photography/Moment Open, Barcroft Media/Barcroft Media, Tom Brakefield/DigitalVision, Tatiane Noviski Fornel/Moment, John M Lund Photography Inc/DigitalVision, Ali Trisno Pranoto/Moment), iStockphoto (AndrewJShearer, EMPPhotography), Minden Pictures (Andy Rouse/NPL, Pierre Vernay/Biosphoto), National Geographic Creative (Michael Nichols, Joel Sartore/National Geographic Photo Ark), Shutterstock (Coffeemill, Lim Yong Hian, hxdbzxy, Eric Isselee, Chansom Pantip, Jan Stria, Popova Valeriya, Wiratchai wansamngam)

Library of Congress Cataloging-in-Publication Data
Names: Gish, Melissa, author.
Title: Tiger / Melissa Gish.
Series: Spotlight on nature.
Includes index.
Summary: A detailed chronology of developmental milestones drives this life study of tigers, including their habitats, physical features, and conservation measures taken to protect these big cats.
Identifiers: LCCN 2018043955 / ISBN 978-1-64026-186-0 (hardcover) / ISBN 978-1-62832-749-6 (pbk) / ISBN 978-1-64000-304-0 (eBook)
Subjects: LCSH: Tiger—Juvenile literature.
Classification: LCC QL737.C23 G5177 2019 / DDC 599.756—dc23

CONTENTS

MEET THE FAMILY

SUMATRAN TIGERS

of the Barisan Mountains

The Barisan Mountains run along the western edge of the island of Sumatra. This mountain range is made up mostly of volcanoes—including 35 that are active. Dense tropical pine forests line the higher slopes. Lower elevations are blanketed with rainforests teeming with wildlife. In southern Sumatra, the Bukit Barisan Selatan National Park covers nearly 1,400 square miles (3,626 sq km) of lowland forest. It is home to many rare animals, such as the Sumatran elephant, Sumatran rhinoceros, and Sumatran tiger.

It is mid-May—the beginning of the dry season—and a balmy 83 °F (28.3 °C). About 100 days ago, a female Sumatran tiger became pregnant. Now she is preparing a place to give birth. She pulls grass and leaves into a pile under a rocky outcropping. This will be her first experience with motherhood. Hidden from view, she lies down on the bed of vegetation and waits.

CLOSE-UP

Eyeshine

Tigers' eyes have a reflective layer of tissue called the tapetum lucidum. This tissue collects light and allows tigers to see six times better than humans in very low light.

CHAPTER ONE

LIFE BEGINS

Tigers are the largest of the world's cat species. Six subspecies exist today. Fewer than 500 Siberian tigers remain in far eastern Russia near the Chinese border. About 2,500 Bengal tigers can be found in India, Bangladesh, Nepal, and Bhutan. Roughly 350 Indochinese tigers live in Myanmar, Thailand, and Laos. About 300 Malayan tigers live in Malaysia. Prior to 2004, it was thought that Indochinese and Malayan tigers were the same, but science has proven that they are different. Found nowhere but on the island for which they are named, around 400 Sumatran tigers exist in the wild. More than 70 South China tigers live in zoos around the world, but this subspecies is believed to be functionally extinct in the wild. Three other subspecies—Caspian, Javan, and Bali tigers—were hunted to extinction by the late 20th century.

BARISAN MOUNTAIN SUMATRAN TIGER MILESTONES

DAY 1

- Born
- Weight (female): 1.8 pounds (0.8 kg)
- Weight (male): 2 pounds (0.9 kg)

FEATURED FAMILY

Welcome to the World

In Bukit Barisan Selatan National Park, the female Sumatran tiger lies on her side. After preparing for five hours, she finally gives birth to her first cub. It is wet and limp. She licks its chest, rousing it to breathe. Then she begins to lick its soft body clean. The female cub cries out, momentarily startling the new mother. A few minutes later, a second cub arrives. This one is male. The tiny cubs are too weak to crawl, so their mother gently pulls them close to her warm body.

Except for females that are raising cubs, tigers live alone in established territories. They spend much of their time roaming their territories. Tigers warn away intruders by marking their territory with urine and deep scratches on trees. Tigers are nocturnal, or most active at night. They have excellent night vision and a powerful sense of smell. These senses are especially useful for hunting. As carnivores, tigers survive by eating meat. Tigers hunt both large and small animals, from deer and wild boars to rabbits and fish.

CLOSE-UP

Sharp tongues

Tigers have small, sharp projections, called papillae, on their tongues. With gentle licks, they can clean their fur. With harder licks, their tongue becomes a grater to scrape meat from bones.

Males meet females only briefly to mate, and they do not take part in raising offspring. Normally, two or three cubs are born. They weigh up to three pounds (1.4 kg), depending on the subspecies. Newborn

2 WEEKS

- Eyes open, and milk teeth emerge
- Drink three ounces (88.7 ml) of milk six times a day
- Weight (female): 3.6 pounds (1.6 kg)
- Weight (male): 4 pounds (1.8 kg)

FEATURED FAMILY

First Meal

The Sumatran tiger cubs are now eight weeks old. It is time for their first taste of prey. Their mother brings them a freshly killed moonrat—a small animal similar to an opossum. The cubs sniff at the moonrat with curiosity. They aren't sure what to do. Their mother rips the animal open. The smell of blood sparks the cubs' instincts. They dive into their first warm, fleshy meal.

cubs' eyes and ears are closed, and they have no teeth. Adult tigers have no natural enemies, but cubs are vulnerable to many predators—including male tigers. For the first two years of life, cubs depend on their mother to protect them. During this time, mothers teach their offspring everything they need to know to survive.

CLOSE-UP

Teeth

Tigers have 30 teeth. Up to three inches (7.6 cm) long, the four canine teeth are used to bite and hold prey. Four sharp carnassials are used like scissors to slice through flesh.

4 WEEKS

- Vision is clear
- Begin exploring den
- Siblings play-wrestle with each other

8 WEEKS

- Leave the den for the first time
- Eating little bits of meat
- Weight (female): 12 pounds (5.4 kg)
- Weight (male): 14.2 pounds (6.4 kg)

CLOSE-UP

Speed and strength

Tigers can sprint up to 37 miles (59.5 km) per hour, but they usually sneak up on prey instead. Thick pads on the bottoms of their feet allow them to creep silently toward prey before pouncing.

CHAPTER TWO

EARLY ADVENTURES

An adult tiger needs 12 pounds (5.4 kg) of meat every day, on average, to survive. Once captured, prey rarely escapes a tiger's jaws. But catching prey is not easy. Only 1 in every 20 attempts is successful. Tigers may go a week without a large meal. When they do catch something big, they may eat up to 75 pounds (34 kg) of meat in one day, hiding the rest for later. Tigers silently stalk prey and kill by surprise. Launched by their powerful hind legs, they pounce on unsuspecting prey. They can also jump 16 feet (4.9 m) straight up to grab prey from trees. These strategies must be learned and practiced. Cubs stalk and pounce on turtles, snakes, bugs, and each other for practice. But they rely on their mothers to feed them for the first two years.

4 MONTHS

- Sharing meals with mother
- Gnawing on bones to strengthen teeth
- Weight (female): 34 pounds (15.4 kg)
- Weight (male): 42.5 pounds (19.3 kg)

Tiger cubs are born toothless. Their first set of teeth, called milk teeth, begin to grow within a week or two. When cubs are about six months old, the milk teeth are gradually pushed out and replaced by stronger permanent teeth. Like all cats, tigers have four toes with retractable claws to grab and hold prey. Tigers scrape trees to sharpen their claws. Cubs practice using their claws to grip and hold everything from leaves and branches to the prey their mothers bring to them. Cubs must learn to use their teeth and jaws, so they often chew on branches.

CLOSE-UP

Matchless markings

No two tigers have the same markings. Like human fingerprints, each tiger's pattern of stripes is unique. The stripes make it difficult for prey animals to spot a tiger's outline in the forest.

FEATURED FAMILY

Look Who's Pouncing

The Sumatran tiger cubs are now almost six months old. About a week ago, their mother smelled a male tiger passing through her territory. She moved her family to a different location. Male tigers may kill cubs they come across. In their new home, the hollow of an enormous tree, the cubs encounter a Malaysian jewel centipede. As the seven-inch-long (17.8 cm) insect races away from the cubs, they give chase. Surrounding the centipede, the cubs take turns stalking and pouncing on it. This play is vital to the cubs' development as hunters. The female cub captures the centipede under one paw but lets it go with a startled yowl when it bites her.

6 MONTHS

- No longer drinking milk
- Practice stalking small prey
- Weight (female): 70 pounds (31.8 kg)
- Weight (male): 80 pounds (36.3 kg)

CLOSE-UP

Vocal communication

Tigers usually roar only to announce their presence to rival tigers in the area. Nervous tigers snarl or make a coughing sound. Relaxed tigers make a sound called a chuffle. It sounds like air blowing through a pipe.

FEATURED FAMILY

Give It a Try

The evening is hotter than usual. The tiger family needs to cool down. The cubs follow their mother to the riverbank. Unlike most other cats, tigers are strong swimmers. They do not shy away from water. The cubs enter the river behind their mother and paddle with their broad paws. They splash playfully. When it's time to go, their mother moans, "Mawww!" The cubs recognize her beckoning voice and paddle for shore. After a good shake, they follow her back into the forest.

Unlike most other cats, **TIGERS** are STRONG *swimmers.*

8 MONTHS

- Permanent teeth are in place
- Learning mother's hunting strategies

CLOSE-UP

Whiskers

Tigers' facial whiskers grow to about six inches (15.2 cm) in length. Whiskers have deep roots connected to **nerves**. They are used to feel surrounding objects and changes in air pressure.

CHAPTER THREE

LIFE LESSONS

Siberian and Bengal tigers are the largest subspecies. Males average 9 to 10 feet (2.7–3 m) long; although they can weigh up to 700 pounds (318 kg), most average 500 to 600 pounds (227–272 kg). Sumatran tigers are the smallest. They are typically about 6.5 feet (2 m) long. Males weigh less than 300 pounds (136 kg). Female tigers are smaller than males. Prey is sparse in Siberian tiger habitat. For this reason, their territories are large, ranging from 320 to 480 square miles (829–1,243 sq km). With more abundant prey, tigers elsewhere can afford to share closer quarters. Their territories vary from 2 to 60 square miles (5.2–155 sq km). A male's territory typically overlaps the smaller territories of three or four females with whom he mates. Males will fight for territory. Younger, stronger males may try to force older males out

1 YEAR

- Confident but unskilled hunters
- Weight (female): 150 pounds (68 kg)
- Weight (male): 200 pounds (90.7 kg)

18 MONTHS

- Capturing some of their own meals
- Siblings become rivals, prepare for independence

CLOSE-UP

Claws

Tigers' claws can be up to four inches (10.2 cm) long. They are curved like hooks and extremely sharp. A protective skin sheath keeps them up off the ground when not being used.

FEATURED FAMILY

This Is How It's Done

In the Barisan Mountains, the Sumatran tiger cubs are a year old. The cubs have grown to nearly 100 times their birth weight. They hide in the brush beside their mother. Close by, a wild boar and her nine offspring snuffle through the soft dirt around a rotting log. These tusked animals can weigh up to 200 pounds (90.7 kg). They fight fiercely when attacked. Suddenly, the mother tiger springs from the brush and grabs one of the young boars. She hurries away with it, and her cubs follow.

SUMATRAN TIGER

SIBERIAN TIGER

of a territory. When a tiger dies, others compete for his territory.

Tigers begin hunting with their mothers at 8 to 10 months old, but they rarely catch prey on their own until they are about 2 years old. By the time a tiger leaves its mother at two to three years old, it will be a skilled hunter and large enough to defend itself against other tigers that it meets while establishing its own territory. Sometimes, a female tiger will allow her female offspring to take over a portion of her own territory. Though it is extremely rare, tigers and their adult offspring have even been known to hunt together.

Male tigers are fully mature at around four to five years of age. Females are mature and can reproduce when they are three to four years

(2) YEARS

- Male leaves to establish his own territory
- Female stays near mother

(4) YEARS

- Female establishes her own territory
- Gives birth to first set of cubs
- Weight: 200 pounds (90.7 kg)

old. A female tiger typically gives birth to a litter of cubs every two years. Only half of all tiger cubs will survive their first two years. Life is challenging for tigers. They face fights with other tigers and risk death from wildfires, flooding, sickness, starvation, and poaching. Most wild tigers do not survive past the age of 12. In captivity, where they are safe and well fed, tigers can live twice that long.

CLOSE-UP

"Eyes" on the ears

Tigers have a white spot on the back of each ear. They show off these spots, called ocelli, by tilting their ears backward. This tells other tigers to back off.

FEATURED FAMILY

Practice Makes Perfect

Now 16 months old, the tigers hide in the tall grass, watching a young sambar deer wander away from its herd. The male tiger, much bigger than his sister, leaps forward and races toward the startled deer. But the deer is quick, and the entire herd disappears into the forest. The tiger gives up. The young Sumatran tigers will continue to practice their hunting skills every day, but they will rely on their mother's help for another six to eight months.

ONLY HALF OF ALL TIGER CUBS WILL SURVIVE THEIR FIRST TWO YEARS.

(5) YEARS

- Male's territory overlaps with two unrelated females
- Becomes a father for the first time
- Weight: 285 pounds (129 kg)

(12) YEARS

- End of lives

CHAPTER FOUR

TIGER SPOTTING

The biggest threats to tigers come from humans. Human expansion into wilderness areas has led to a decline in large prey animals, such as deer and boars. Tigers may be forced to turn to livestock for food. About 85 people are also killed or injured by tigers annually. Experts believe the tigers simply mistake people for prey. Perceived problem tigers are often killed by fearful villagers. In 1996, Indonesian businessman Tomy Winata founded the Tambling Wildlife Nature Conservation. It includes about 119,000 acres (48,158 ha) of protected forest in Sumatra. Within the area is a rescue center for Sumatran tigers. Experts capture "conflict tigers" (those that have attacked people) and teach them to fear and stay away from humans. Injured tigers are also rehabilitated. The tigers are then released into the protected forest.

The Smithsonian's National Zoo in Washington, D.C., features Sumatran tigers and a Siberian tiger named Pavel. Because the zoo's Sumatran tiger-breeding program has been successful, the zoo hopes to begin breeding Siberian tigers as well. The Minnesota Zoo already has a successful breeding program in place for Siberian (or Amur) tigers. Zoo visitors can see Sundari, born at the zoo in 2012, and her offspring, Vera, born in 2017.

Since the San Diego Zoo began its tiger conservation program in 1988 and was joined in 2014 by the San Diego Zoo Safari Park, more than 100 Bengal, Malayan, Siberian, and Sumatran tigers have been born at the facilities. Visitors to the zoo's website can watch Sumatran tigers on the live Tiger Cam. The Woodland Park Zoo in Seattle, Washington, also has a Web cam on its Malayan tiger exhibit. This zoo works with Panthera, a wild cat conservation organization, to study the tigers in their native Malaysia.

For thousands of years, tigers have been valued for their fur and body parts, which are used in some traditional medicines. Tigers have been hunted nearly to extinction. While more than 5,000 tigers live in zoos around the world, only about 3,200 remain in the wild. Although many zoos participate in breeding programs, few tigers raised in captivity have been successfully released into the wild. The only sure way to save tigers is to save the forests and wetlands they inhabit. Scientists hope to preserve tiger populations long enough to discover lasting solutions that will ensure that tigers survive long into the future.

FAMILY ALBUM

SNAPSHOTS

On June 27, 2016, twin **Sumatran tigers** Achilles and Karis were born at the London Zoo. The zoo participates in a Global Species Management Programme for **Sumatran tigers**.

Mohan, a white **Bengal tiger**, was captured as a cub in India in 1951. He is believed to be the forefather of all white tigers born in captivity to this day.

About 250 of the world's **Indochinese tigers** live in Thailand. The rest, fewer than 100 individuals, live in Myanmar and Laos.

Only about 120 **Malayan tigers** of breeding age exist in scattered forests and swamps of southern Malaysia, where they prey mainly on sambar deer.

SITA

Sita was a **Bengal tiger** living in India's Bandhavgarh National Park. In 1997, she was featured in *National Geographic* magazine. She was killed by poachers a year later.

By the 1940s, overhunting left only about 50 **Siberian tigers** in the wild. Then the Russian government took steps to protect them. Their population has now increased to nearly 500 wild individuals.

Because they live in a cold climate, **Siberian tigers** have a layer of insulating fat under their skin. Their fur is longer and thicker than that of their tropical cousins.

In the 1980s, fewer than 40 **South China tigers** remained in the wild. When scientists searched for them in 2001, they found no signs of the tigers.

Siberian tigers are also known as **Amur tigers**. Declining food sources have led this subspecies to develop smaller bodies in recent decades—typically around 400 pounds (181 kg) today.

With fewer than 400 **Sumatran tigers** left, scientists fear this tiger subspecies may go the way of its extinct relatives, the **Bali** and **Javan tigers**.

A **Bengal tiger** named Machli (or Machali) lived in India's Ranthambore National Park for 19 years. Park rangers fed Machli in her old age and gave her a traditional Hindu funeral when she died.

The decline of large prey animals has forced the **Indochinese tiger** to hunt smaller prey such as monkeys and muntjac. Without sufficient food, tigers cannot reproduce.

The **Indochinese tiger's** fur differs slightly from that of its cousins. The orange color is darker than most, and the stripes are narrower.

WORDS to Know

captivity — living in a place from which escape is not possible

extinct — died off completely; having no living members

nerves — fibers that carry sensations to the brain and impulses from the brain to other body parts

poaching — hunting protected species of wild animals, even though doing so is against the law

rectractable — able to be drawn back in from an extended position

species — a group of living beings with shared characteristics and the ability to reproduce with one another

territories — areas owned or claimed and defended from intruders

LEARN MORE

Books

Marsh, Laura. *Tigers*. Washington, D.C.: National Geographic, 2012.

Simon, Seymour. *Big Cats*. Rev. ed. New York: HarperCollins, 2017.

Winter, Steve, and Sharon Guynup. *Tigers Forever: Saving the World's Most Endangered Big Cat*. Washington, D.C.: National Geographic, 2013.

Websites

"Tiger." National Geographic Kids. https://kids.nationalgeographic.com/animals/mammals/tiger/.

"Tiger." San Diego Zoo Kids. https://kids.sandiegozoo.org/animals/tiger.

"Where Do Tigers Live? And Other Tiger Facts." WWF. https://www.worldwildlife.org/stories/where-do-tigers-live-and-other-tiger-facts.

Documentaries

Meade, Craig. *The Miracle Tiger*. 6 episodes. NHNZ, 2015.

Rahman, Harun. *Sumatra's Last Tigers*. Mediacorp Private Ltd., 2015.

Tourell, Wayne, and Richard Thomas. *Tigers: Fighting Back*. NHNZ, 2016.

Visit

CAROLINA TIGER RESCUE

Provides a home and care for big cats rescued from exploitation.

1940 Hanks Chapel Road
Pittsboro, NC 27312

JUNGLE CAT WORLD

Safari Zoo Camp allows summer campers to witness night feedings of tigers.

3667 Concession Road 6
Orono, ON
Canada L08 1M0

MINNESOTA ZOO

Coordinates the Tiger Species Survival Plan for zoos and aquariums across North America.

13000 Zoo Boulevard
Apple Valley, MN 55124

THE WILD ANIMAL SANCTUARY

This 9,793-acre (3,963 ha) refuge provides for more than 500 lions, tigers, and other large carnivores.

2999 County Road 53
Keenseburg, CO 80643

INDEX